Transgender Romance

140 MUST-ASK QUESTIONS BEFORE DATING TRANSGENDER WOMEN

DISCLAIMER

This book is designed to provide information only. This information is provided and sold with the knowledge that the publisher and author do not offer any legal or other professional advice. In the case of a need for any such expertise, consult with the appropriate professional.

This book does not contain all the information available on the subject. This book has not been created to be specific to any individual's or organization's situation or needs. Every effort has been made to make this book as accurate as possible. However, there may be typographical and or content errors. Therefore, this book should serve only as a general guide, not as the ultimate source of subject information.

This book contains information that might be dated and is intended only to educate and entertain. The author and publisher shall have no liability or responsibility to any person or entity regarding any loss or damage incurred or alleged to have incurred, directly or indirectly, by the information contained in this book.

Table of Contents

The Ultimate List Of Must Ask Questions Before Dating A Transgender Woman

Introduction

Hey there! Are you considering dating a transgender woman as a straight guy? Congratulations on taking the time to educate yourself with these critical questions that may arise in such a relationship.

Dating a transgender woman can be a rewarding and fulfilling experience, but it's important to approach the relationship with care, respect, and understanding. That's why I wrote this book – to provide you with a comprehensive list of questions to ask yourself before entering into a relationship with a transgender woman.

From values and family dynamics, to sex and social issues, this book covers a wide range of topics that may impact your relationship with a transgender woman. By considering these questions before starting a relationship, you'll be better equipped to navigate any potential challenges or conflicts and build a strong and healthy relationship based on mutual understanding and respect.

Of course, every relationship is unique, and these questions are just a starting point. It's important to approach each question with an open and curious mindset and to communicate openly and respectfully with your partner throughout the relationship.

So, whether you're just starting to explore the possibility of dating a transgender woman or are already in a relationship and looking to strengthen your connection, this book will provide the tools you need to build a healthy and fulfilling relationship.

Good luck!

Why this a book is necessary?

You're curious about why a book on "Questions You Must Ask Yourself Before Dating a Transgender Woman" is important, right? Well, buckle up, because we're about to dive into the reasons why this book is not only important but essential for the modern dating world.

First, let's acknowledge that society has evolved significantly in recent years, with more and more people becoming open and accepting of diverse gender identities. And you know what? That's fantastic! But, as with anything new, there can be some confusion and misunderstandings. That's where this book comes in, to guide you through the process and ensure you're ready for a healthy, loving relationship with a transgender woman.

Why does this matter? Well, dating a transgender woman can be a beautiful and fulfilling experience. However, it's crucial to be aware of your own beliefs, biases, and expectations before diving in. The book helps you reflect on your own feelings and attitudes, ensuring that you're coming from a place of love and understanding.

One key aspect the book covers is the need to educate yourself on transgender issues. It's not fair to expect your partner to be your sole source of information on all things trans-related. However, by asking yourself the right questions and seeking answers, you'll be better equipped to support your partner and create a strong foundation for your relationship.

Moreover, the book helps you explore your own motivations for wanting to date a transgender woman. Are you genuinely attracted to her and want to build a life together? Or are you simply intrigued by the "exotic" or "taboo" aspects of her identity? Knowing the answers to these questions is vital in ensuring you're not fetishizing or objectifying your partner.

Lastly, the book emphasizes the importance of communication, trust, and respect in any relationship. Encouraging self-reflection helps you cultivate the empathy and understanding needed to foster a supportive, loving partnership.

So, there you have it! This book is crucial because it promotes self-awareness, fosters empathy, and contributes to a more inclusive, understanding dating landscape. By asking yourself the right questions, you'll be better prepared to embark on a meaningful, lasting relationship with a transgender woman. So, go forth and love with an open heart and an open mind!

How to use this book?

We're thrilled that you're interested in this incredible book. And guess what? You don't have to read it cover to cover like a traditional novel. Nope! This gem is designed to be your trusty companion as you navigate the world of dating transgender women.

So, how do you make the most of this book? Easy peasy! Just flip to the section that tickles your fancy or fits your current mood or mindset. Each topic is organized to give you the lowdown on what's essential, so you can get the info you need without any fuss. We know life can get hectic, and this book is here to make things easier for you.

Are you feeling curious about understanding transgender issues? Head on over to that section and soak up the knowledge! Maybe you're in the mood to reflect on your motivations and feelings; there's a section for that too! Communication and trust-building tips? We've got you covered.

The beauty of this book lies in its flexibility, allowing you to jump in and out as needed. It's like having a wise best friend by your side, ready to offer guidance, insight, and support whenever you need it. So whether you're lounging on the couch, waiting for your morning coffee, or taking a quick break at work, you can always find a relevant section to explore.

Remember, the journey of self-discovery and growth is not a one-size-fits-all experience. Feel free to move at your own pace and revisit topics whenever needed. After all, you're the captain of your own ship, and this book is your trusty compass, guiding you toward a deeper understanding and a more meaningful connection with the transgender woman in your life.

Happy reading, and cheers to making the most of this fantastic resource!

The Ultimate List Of Must Ask Questions Before Dating A Transgender Woman

Expectations

1. Are you open to learning about transgender experiences and identities?

2. Can you listen to and respect your partner's boundaries and needs?

3. Do you understand the potential risks and challenges of dating a transgender woman (like discrimination and transphobia)?

4. Are you comfortable with your sexuality and able to communicate your desires and boundaries effectively?

5. Do you have any prejudices or biases that could affect how you treat your partner?

6. Will you stand up for your partner and their rights if needed?

7. Have you educated yourself about the physical and emotional changes trans people may go through during transition?

8. Do you understand that not all trans women want or can afford gender-affirming surgeries or hormone therapy?

9. Can you respect your partner's preferred name and pronouns, even if it takes some time to get used to them?

10. Do you see your partner as a whole person, beyond just being a "transgender woman"?

Values

1. Do you value honesty and openness in a relationship, and are you willing to share your feelings and thoughts?

2. Do you treat everyone with respect and kindness, regardless of their gender identity?

3. Do you value empathy and understanding, and can you put yourself in your partner's shoes?

4. Are you supportive of individuality and self-expression, and can you accept your partner's gender identity without judgment?

5. Do you believe in equality and social justice, and will you stand up against discrimination and bigotry toward trans people?

6. Do you value communication and actively work to improve your skills in this area?

7. Are you open to personal growth and development, and willing to learn and grow alongside your partner?

8. Will you support your partner's goals and dreams, and be a partner who encourages and empowers them?

9. Do you value diversity and inclusivity, and will you appreciate the unique qualities your partner brings to the relationship?

10. Do you prioritize consent and respecting boundaries, and will you put your partner's needs and desires first?

Religion

1. Does your religion teach you to accept and love everyone regardless of gender identity?

2. Are you okay with dating someone who may have different beliefs or religious practices than you do?

3. Does your religion have any teachings about gender identity that could impact your relationship with a transgender woman?

4. Are you open to respectful dialogue about religion and spirituality with your partner?

5. Does your religion teach you to value forgiveness and compassion, and can you extend these values to your partner?

6. Will you respect your partner's religious beliefs and practices, even if they differ from yours?

7. Does your religion encourage you to stand up for the rights and dignity of all people, including marginalized individuals?

8. Are you willing to handle any potential conflicts in religious beliefs with your partner respectfully and constructively?

9. Does your religion emphasize mutual respect and consent in relationships, and can you uphold these values with your partner?

10. Are you open to learning and growing in your understanding of gender and sexuality, even if it challenges your preconceived notions?

Family

1. Do you have a supportive and accepting family, or are you worried about their reaction to you dating a transgender woman?

2. Are you willing to discuss your relationship openly with your family and defend your partner if needed?

3. Do you think your family's opinions should influence your decision to date a transgender woman?

4. Are you willing to set boundaries with your family if they're not supportive or disrespectful towards your partner?

5. Have you considered how your partner may feel about meeting your family, and will you support them in potentially challenging situations?

6. Do you value your family's input and opinions, and are you open to hearing their concerns or questions about your relationship with a transgender woman?

7. Have you educated yourself about the experiences and challenges trans people may face in family relationships?

8. Will you prioritize your partner's emotional and physical safety, even if it means distancing yourself from unsupportive or harmful family members?

9. Have you considered how dating a transgender woman might affect your future family plans, and are you open to discussing these

Friendship

1. Do you have friends who support and accept LGBTQ+ people, and are you comfortable introducing your partner to them?

2. Will you stand up for your partner if your friends make insensitive comments about trans people?

3. Have you thought about how your friendships might change when dating a transgender woman?

4. Do you value friendships built on open communication, empathy, and mutual respect?

5. Are you willing to make room in your life for your partner, even if it means adjusting your social calendar or activities?

6. Have you learned about the experiences and challenges trans people face in friendships and social settings?

7. Do you believe friendships should be based on shared values and respect for everyone, regardless of gender identity?

8. Will you prioritize your partner's emotional and physical safety, even if it means distancing yourself from unsupportive or harmful friends?

9. Have you thought about how dating a transgender woman might impact your friendships with straight cis men, and are you open to discussing these topics with them?

10. Do you think friendships are important, but also recognize that your relationship with your partner should be based on mutual love and respect?

Social life

1. Are you comfortable being seen in public with a transgender woman and willing to stand up against potential harassment or discrimination?

2. Do you believe your social life should be based on mutual respect and inclusivity, and are you willing to educate your friends about trans issues?

3. Have you thought about how your social life might change when dating a transgender woman?

4. Are you willing to make room in your life for your partner, even if it means adjusting your social calendar or activities?

5. Have you learned about the experiences and challenges trans people face in social settings?

6. Do you believe your social life should reflect your values, including support for the LGBTQ+ community?

7. Will you prioritize your partner's emotional and physical safety, even if it means distancing yourself from unsupportive or harmful social circles?

8. Have you thought about how dating a transgender woman might impact your interactions with straight cis men, and are you open to discussing these topics with them?

9. Do you think social connections and community are important, but also recognize that your relationship with your partner should be based on mutual love and respect?

10. Are you willing to work on building a supportive and inclusive social life with your partner and strive for a more accepting world for everyone, regardless of their gender identity?

Mental health

1. Are you emotionally ready for a relationship and in a stable, healthy mental state?

2. Have you considered how your mental health might impact your ability to support and care for your partner?

3. Will you prioritize your partner's emotional needs and support them through any mental health challenges they may face?

4. Have you learned about the mental health experiences and challenges trans people may face?

5. Are you willing to provide a safe and supportive space for your partner to express themselves and seek help if needed?

6. Do you value open and honest communication, and are you willing to discuss mental health with your partner while actively listening to their needs?

7. Have you considered how your partner's mental health might impact your relationship and are you willing to be patient and understanding during difficult times?

8. Will you seek help and support if you need it and take care of both your mental health and your partner's?

9. Do you believe in the importance of mental health and self-care, and are you willing to prioritize these aspects in your life and relationship?

10. Will you support your partner in seeking mental health care or therapy, and help them navigate potential challenges or barriers?

Sexuality

1. Have you educated yourself about the anatomy and sexual experiences of trans women, and are you willing to approach sex with an open and curious mindset?

2. Will you prioritize your partner's comfort and pleasure during sex, and communicate openly about desires and boundaries?

3. Have you considered how your own sexual experiences and desires might change when dating a transgender woman?

4. Are you willing to explore different sexual activities that may be more pleasurable or comfortable for your partner and learn from their feedback and guidance?

5. Do you value consent and communication, and are you willing to actively listen to your partner's needs and desires during sexual experiences?

6. Have you educated yourself about the potential risks and benefits of various sexual practices?

7. Are you willing to approach any potential sexual challenges with patience, understanding, and a willingness to seek outside help or resources if necessary?

8. Have you considered how your partner's past experiences with sex and intimacy may impact your relationship, and are you willing to provide emotional support and understanding if needed?

9. Do you understand that not all trans women may be comfortable or interested in certain sexual activities, and are you willing to respect your partner's boundaries and desires?

10. Are you willing to prioritize mutual respect, pleasure, and communication in all aspects of your sexual relationship, and to work collaboratively with your partner to create a fulfilling and satisfying sexual experience for both of you?

Surgery

1. Do you understand the different types of gender-affirming surgeries that trans people may undergo, and are you comfortable with the idea of your partner potentially having surgery?

2. Are you willing to support your partner through any surgical procedures or recovery periods they may have?

3. Have you educated yourself about the potential risks and benefits of gender-affirming surgeries?

4. Do you believe in the importance of bodily autonomy and self-determination, and are you willing to respect your partner's decisions regarding their own body?

5. Are you comfortable with the potential changes that may occur in your partner's body due to surgery or hormone therapy?

6. Have you considered how your partner's surgical history or current plans may impact your sexual experiences or intimacy?

7. Do you value communication and transparency in a relationship, and are you willing to have ongoing discussions about your partner's surgical experiences and needs?

8. Are you willing to provide emotional and physical support to your partner through any surgical procedures or recovery periods they may have?

9. Have you considered how your partner's surgical history or current plans may impact their overall health and well-being, and are you willing to support them in seeking any necessary medical care?

10. Do you understand that not all trans people choose to undergo gender-affirming surgeries, and can you respect your partner's decisions and needs regardless of their surgical history or plans?

Children

1. Do you want to have children in the future, and have you discussed this topic with your partner?

2. Have you considered how your partner's gender identity may impact your plans for starting a family, and are you willing to be flexible and creative in exploring different options for parenting?

3. Are you willing to support your partner through any potential challenges or discrimination they may face as a trans parent or co-parent?

4. Have you educated yourself about the experiences and challenges that trans parents may face, and are you willing to advocate for and support your partner in these areas?

5. Do you value open and honest communication about parenting and family planning, and are you willing to have ongoing discussions with your partner about these topics?

6. Have you considered how your partner's gender identity may impact your interactions with other parents or caregivers, and are you willing to support your partner through any potential challenges in these areas?

7. Are you willing to prioritize your partner's emotional and physical needs during the parenting process?

8. Have you considered how your own gender identity or expectations of traditional gender roles may impact your parenting dynamic, and are you willing to approach parenting as a collaborative and equal partnership?

9. Do you believe in the importance of creating a safe, inclusive, and affirming environment for any potential children you may have, and are you willing to work collaboratively with your partner to create this environment?

10. Are you willing to prioritize your family unit and the well-being of any potential children you may have, and to make any necessary adjustments or sacrifices to support their growth and development?

Politics

1. Do you have political beliefs that support LGBTQ+ rights and inclusivity, and are you willing to advocate for and support your partner in these areas?

2. Have you educated yourself about the political issues and challenges that trans people may face, and are you willing to be an ally and advocate for these issues?

3. Are you willing to have open and honest conversations with your partner about your political beliefs and values, and to listen and learn from their perspective?

4. Do you believe in the importance of social justice and equity, and are you willing to prioritize these values in your own life and your relationship?

5. Have you considered how your political beliefs and affiliations may impact your relationship, and are

you willing to navigate any potential disagreements or conflicts respectfully and understandingly?

6. Are you willing to use your privilege and platform as a straight cis man to amplify the voices and experiences of marginalized communities, including the trans community?

7. Have you considered how your partner's experiences with discrimination and marginalization may impact their political beliefs and perspectives, and are you willing to provide emotional support and understanding in these areas?

8. Do you believe in the importance of voting and civic engagement, and are you willing to participate in political action and advocacy alongside your partner?

9. Have you considered how your political beliefs and actions may impact your future plans and

goals as a couple, and are you willing to have ongoing discussions about these topics?

10. Are you willing to prioritize your relationship, mutual love, and respect over any potential political disagreements or conflicts?

Social Issues

1. Have you familiarized yourself with the social issues and challenges that trans people may face, such as discrimination, violence, and lack of access to healthcare?

2. Are you willing to use your privilege and platform as a straight cis man to advocate for and support the rights and needs of marginalized communities, including the trans community?

3. Have you considered how your own social identity and experiences may impact your ability to understand and empathize with your partner's experiences as a trans person?

4. Are you willing to listen and learn from your partner's experiences and perspectives, and to actively work to dismantle any internalized biases or prejudices you may hold?

5. Have you educated yourself about the history and experiences of the LGBTQ+ rights movement, and are you willing to participate in activism and advocacy alongside your partner?

6. Do you believe in the importance of creating inclusive and affirming spaces for all individuals, regardless of their gender identity or expression?

7. Are you willing to stand up to any potential discrimination or harassment your partner may face in social situations, and to provide emotional support and understanding throughout these experiences?

8. Have you considered how your own social circle and community may react to your relationship with a transgender woman, and are you willing to navigate any potential challenges or conflicts in a respectful and understanding manner?

9. Are you willing to prioritize open and honest communication about any potential social

challenges or concerns that may arise in your relationship, and to work collaboratively with your partner to find solutions?

10. Do you believe in the importance of building a more just, equitable, and inclusive society? Are you willing to participate in this work alongside your partner and other members of marginalized communities?

Future Plans

1. Have you considered your own long-term goals and plans, and how a potential relationship with a transgender woman may impact these plans?

2. Are you willing to be flexible and adaptable in your future plans to accommodate the needs and desires of your partner?

3. Have you discussed your future plans with your partner, and are you willing to prioritize open and honest communication about your individual and shared goals?

4. Have you considered how your partner's own goals and aspirations may impact your future plans as a couple, and are you willing to support and encourage their growth and development?

5. Are you willing to work collaboratively with your partner to create a shared vision for your future as

a couple, and to make any necessary adjustments or sacrifices to achieve these goals?

6. Have you considered how your future plans may impact your financial situation, and are you willing to be open and transparent about your finances and financial goals?

7. Do you believe in the importance of creating a safe, supportive, and inclusive home environment for your future together, and are you willing to prioritize this goal in your future plans?

8. Have you considered how your future plans may impact your social circle and community?

9. Have you considered how your own values and priorities may evolve and shift over time, and are you willing to approach your future plans with an open and flexible mindset?

Conclusion

Well, folks, we've reached the end of our enlightening journey together with this book, "Questions You Must Ask Yourself Before Dating a Transgender Woman."

We've covered a lot of ground, shared some laughs, and hopefully, you've gained valuable insights along the way. So, let's wrap this up with some heartfelt takeaways, shall we?

At its core, this book is all about fostering love, understanding, and respect for ourselves and our partners. Of course, dating a transgender woman, like any relationship, comes with its own set of challenges and rewards.

But by asking yourself the right questions, you're laying the foundation for a beautiful, meaningful connection that transcends labels and stereotypes.

Remember, the most important aspects of any relationship are communication, trust, and empathy. By taking the time to truly understand your own motivations, beliefs, and expectations, you're better equipped to support your partner and create a loving, safe space for both of you to flourish.

So, as you embark on this incredible journey of dating and self-discovery, always remember to approach it with an open heart and an open mind. Be honest with yourself, be kind to your partner, and above all, respect their individuality and experiences.

The world of love and relationships is ever-evolving, and it's an exciting time to be a part of it! Embrace the opportunity to learn, grow, and love in all its beautiful forms. Here's to you and your future adventures in the vast, wonderful world of dating. Cheers!

I need your help, and here is why.

Hey there, lovely readers! So, you've just heard all about the awesomeness of this book, "Questions You Must Ask Yourself Before Dating a Transgender Woman," and I'm guessing you're as excited about it as I am.

Now, how about we help each other out and spread the word to even more people? Yep, you got it—by leaving a review!

You see, reviews are like little nuggets of gold for both authors and readers alike. They give folks like you the chance to share your thoughts on the book and let others know just how valuable it is.

Plus, they help authors (like yours truly) reach a wider audience, so more people can benefit from the book's message.

So, let's do each other a solid, shall we? Once you've read the book, head on over to your favorite online book retailer and drop a line or two about what you thought.

It doesn't have to be a literary masterpiece, just an honest and friendly note about what you loved, what you learned, or how the book has impacted your perspective on dating and relationships.

By leaving a review, not only are you helping me (thanks, by the way!), but you're also making it easier for others to discover this vital message. In addition, you'll be contributing to a more open, empathetic, and understanding dating world, and honestly, who wouldn't want that?

So, grab your keyboard or your phone, and let's get those reviews rolling! I appreciate your support, and I'm sure future readers will too.

Together, we can make a difference and spread love, one reader at a time. Happy reviewing!

—Please leave a review!

As always, we value your feedback and would love to read your review of this book!